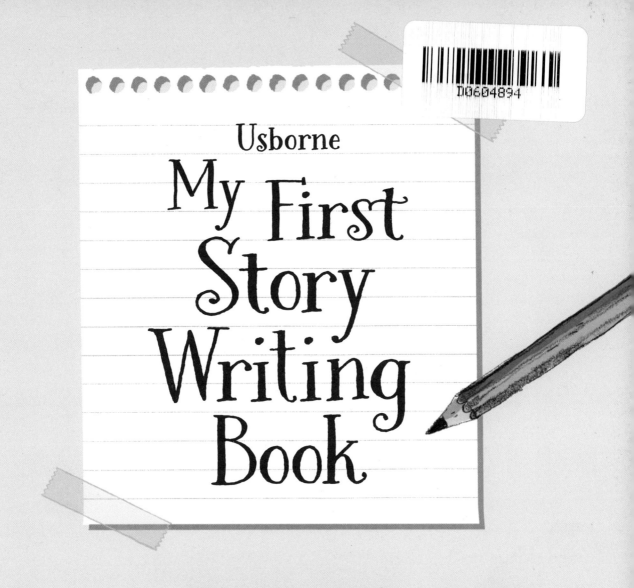

Usborne
My First Story Writing Book

With stories written by

Write your name here.

What's in this book?

That's you!

There are spaces throughout the book for your own writing.

You'll find lots of useful tips along the way.

Action!

Beginnings, middles, endings and titles

Story planning and ideas

The second half of the book has room for longer stories.

About the author

Imagine that one day you're a world-famous author.
Tell your fans a little about yourself here.

My full name is

....

....

Some authors have made-up names, called 'pen names'.

My signature looks like this

....

I live with

....

....

....

....

The most unusual thing about me is

....

....

....

My worst fear is

....

....

....

....

....

I feel
happy when

....

....

....

....

My biggest ambition is

....

....

....

....

....

....

My first memory is

....

....

....

Mix and match

Draw lines to match each word with
the picture it best describes.

tuneful   talented   sneaky   magic

Now draw lines to match each describing word with a thing.

Playing games
with words helps
get you ready to
write stories.

Describing words	Things
delightful	monster
hairy	cucumber
SHOCKED	telephone
horrible	jewel
surprised	policeman
priceless	umbrella
sparkling	ice cream
ENORMOUS	elephant

Use phrases from the boxes below to complete this description of an exciting invention.

I've invented ....
Choose a description from box A.

way to ....
Choose a phrase from box B.

And guess what, it ....
Choose a phrase from box C.

A

the fastest
the easiest
an invisible
a silent
a solar-powered

B

brush your teeth
bake a cake
flush the toilet
reach the moon
win a race

C

works underwater.
runs on honey.
takes two seconds.
glows in the dark.
never breaks.

What are you
going to call
your invention?
....
....

7

Surprise party

Imagine you're planning a party that's full of surprises. What strange things might you buy?

The surprises can be yucky or yummy.

Shopping List
- creepy-crawly cupcakes
- slime green sauce

aa-choo!

stinky

I like mud pies sprinkled with pepper.

Write a cake recipe for the party by filling in the spaces below with some unusual ingredients.

Recipe

Mix together ....

.... and

....

Whisk in ....

....

Bake for one hour. ....

Decorate with ....

....

Give the cake a name.

....

Draw what it looks like.

gold flakes   hair-raising flour

orange peel   eye of newt

sliced turnips   chocolate chips

dried seaweed   gooey ice cream

Here are some ideas.

Speech bubbles

What's going on in these pictures? Fill in words for the characters to say or noises for them to make.

These shapes are called speech bubbles.

ROOOAAARRRR!   I'm starving.   HELP!   I'll spike you!

Weeble zod fla.   Fair maiden!   Hello.   I'll save you.   11

Thinking up characters

Here are some characters. What do you think they are like? How would you describe them to someone else?

Make up names for the characters. There are some ideas on the right-hand page.

She's very ....
....
....

She likes to ....
....

Name:
Maddy Muckabout

Name:
....

She can ....
....
....

Name:
....

He makes ....
....

Name ideas

1. You could give your character a title.

Lady   Captain   Sir   Professor   Mr.   Mrs.

2. Choose a first name or a nickname.

Bob   Clarissa   Whiskers   Joy   Wheelie

3. Make up a last name.

Smiler   Moonface   Spottychops   Heavyfeet   Bubble

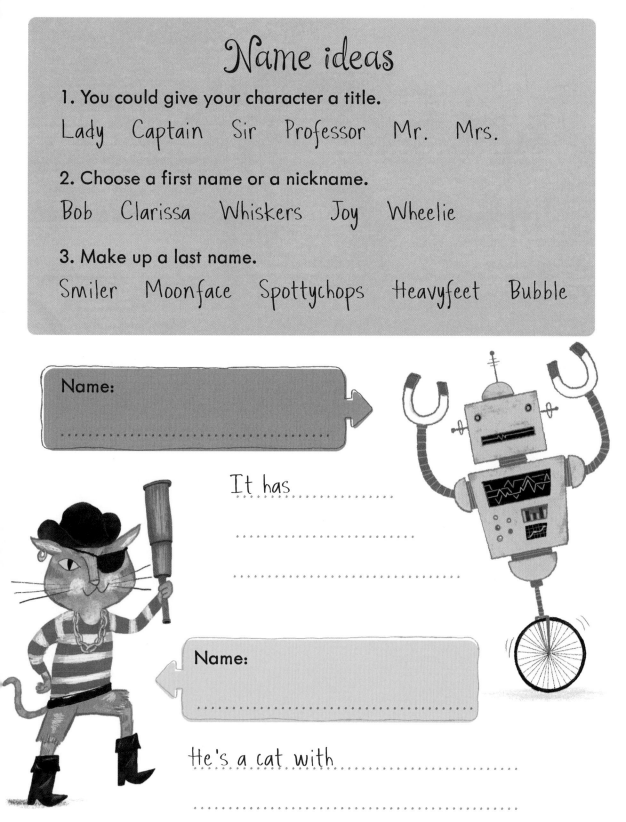

Name: ....

It has ....

....

....

Name: ....

He's a cat with ....

....

Inside their heads

Guess what these characters are thinking and how they are feeling. Maybe someone's hiding a secret...

I wish ....
....

Why is this girl excited?

....
....

Woof ....
....
....

This man is worried because
....
....

Write some words for his song.

....

....

....

....

I'm looking forward to ....

....

What a curious song.

STATION EXIT

FRAGILE

What's inside this package?

....

....

15

Doodle a character

Draw different features on these faces using the doodles below for ideas. Describe their features in the boxes.

pixie ears

Big nose?
Cheesy grin?
Take your pick!

Who could this be? Doodle on features and clothes and write what the character is saying.

I'm ....
....
....

You could add a bag or a pet.

Write about your character here. What makes him or her happy, excited, upset, worried?

....
....
....
....
....

show-off

dreamer

SHY

enigmatic smile

scrawny legs

doodle dragon

bushy eyebrows

angelic

TOOTHLESS GRIN

dangly earrings

inquisitive

Diary story

Pick one of these characters and fill in a page of his or her diary.

I'll never go to the ball.

It's very hot today.

I'm an awesome spy.

Cinderella

A rock star

An Egyptian pharaoh

Secret Agent Raccoon

A superhero

Date ....

Dear Diary,

This morning, I ....
....
....

Then a surprising thing happened – ....
....
....

Later in the day, I discovered ....
....
....

At bedtime, I ....
....
....

My Diary

TOP SECRET

Describing things

Using describing words helps to bring your stories to life.
What words would you use to describe these things?

A monster could be...

1. ....
2. ....
3. ....
4. ....
5. ....
6. ....

A snake could be...

1. ....
2. ....
3. ....
4. ....
5. ....
6. ....

A knight could be...

1. ....
2. ....
3. ....
4. ....
5. ....
6. ....

noisy **hungry** slithering **strong** noble

How would you describe
this boy's bedroom?

His bedroom is ....
....
It has ....
....
....

How about these princesses?

The princesses are ....
....
....
They have ....
....
....
....

stubborn   **LOUD**   pointy   smelly   messy   21

What's it like?

A fun way to describe characters or things is to compare them with something or someone else.

Do you have a friend who can climb like me? Write his or her name here.

.... climbs like a monkey.

Join up these lines to make the best descriptions.

Her eyes sparkled   like a baby.
He sniffed the air   like cotton balls.
She cried   like diamonds.
The clouds are   like thunder.
His voice boomed   like a dog.

Think of ways to finish these sentences and fill them in.

Her legs wobbled like ....

The sea shimmered like ....

His stomach rumbled like ....

Match words from each list to make some more comparisons.

How would you describe me?

The fairy is	as light	as a cloud.
The flowers were	as white	as snow.
The sheep was	as fluffy	as a feather.

Now try describing yourself.

My hair is as ....

as ....

My eyes are like ....

....

My nose is ....

....

Create a scene

Imagine you're writing a story about yourself.
Where are you?

Use this space
to sketch what's
around you.

Now describe where you are.

. . . .

. . . .

. . . .

. . . .

. . . .

Imagine yourself in these places.

What would the views be like?

What goes on in these buildings?

Does anyone else live here?

25

How does it feel?

There's more to a place than
what it *looks* like...

towering

Imagine you are in this forest.
What can you hear?

....

....

What can you smell?

....

....

What might be hiding in the shadows?

....

....

prickly

ROTTEN

sweet-scented

damp

rustling

enchanted

lost

wispy

shadowy

How does it make you feel?

· ·

· ·

What happens next?

· ·

· ·

· ·

· ·

· ·

creak

hooting

Hidden in the forest
are some describing
words that might
help you.

mysterious

spine-tingling

whispering

soft

Mystery box

Don't open this box. There's something very secret inside.

What do you think is inside? Is it a nice secret?

Uh oh! The box falls and bursts open. What happens next?

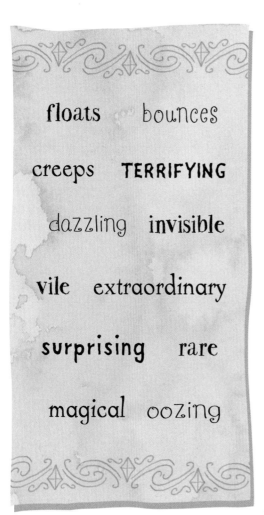

floats   bounces

creeps   **TERRIFYING**

dazzling   **invisible**

vile   extraordinary

surprising   rare

magical   oozing

....

....

....

....

....

....

....

....

....

Ooo... spooky!

Can you fill in this spooky
story and make someone shiver?

One dark, dark night ....

....

It sounded like ....

....

Through the gloom came ....

....

Suddenly ....

....

By sunrise, ...

....

....

Often the
spookiest things aren't
the ones you can *see*,
but the things you can
hear or feel.

tickling   BOO!

creepy   *shadowy*   eery

sudden   twit-twoo   silently

GHOSTLY   out of nowhere

Action story

Fill in the blanks to create an action-packed story.
What does the explorer do? How does she escape?

The explorer saw a massive lion ....
.... after her. She
.... and then she
....
She felt ....

You could use a few
of the action words
below in your story.

hid   rolled   **heard**   riding   creeping
bounding   **ducked**   YELLED   swimming

Just then, the lion ....
....
so the explorer had to ....
.... and then she
....
Luckily ....
.... until at last she
....
....
and the lion ....
....
....

explode   *leaping*   **crawling**   ROARING

screamed   backflipped   **threw**   31

Just do it

If you could do anything in the world, what would you do?

1. ....

....

2. ....

....

3. ....

....

4. ....

....

If I could do anything, I'd go into space.

Action word ideas

invent

create

buy   FIGHT   play

find   become   run

eat

fly   travel   speak   dive   sing

act   explore   ride   perform   meet

Now write a story about doing
one of the things on your list.

One glorious day, I ....

....

....

I couldn't believe it when ....

....

....

My hands shook as ....

....

....

That evening, I felt completely ....

....

....

What next?

Write what happens next to the characters in these two stories.

sneeze

SNORT

tripped

soar

ROARED

swooped

perched

feed

rode

There once was a boy who found a lost dragon wandering behind his school. He decided to

But the dragon

So

34

ERUPTED

plummeted

steered

jumped

crashed

landed

whirled

sighed

parachuted

Agent K was flying past a volcano when it
began to erupt, so she ....
....
....
....
....
Finally, ...
....
....
....

Pick and mix

Stories can be about ANYTHING. Pick any three cards on this page and make a story out of them.

fan

banana

treasure map

ballerina

guitar

Grandpa

jellyfish

teapot

Here's an example:

baseball bat

apple

penguin

juice millionaire

Which three cards have you chosen?

1. ....

2. ....

and 3. ....

You could tell your story out loud first, before you write it down.

Now write your story here.

There was once ....

....

....

....

....

....

....

....

....

Beginnings

There are lots of ways to start a story.
Try writing some first lines.

Fairy tales often start with these words.

Once upon a time there lived ....

....

Long ago, there was ....

....

Many stories begin by describing a scene.

It was dawn, and the birds ....

....

The sea ....

....

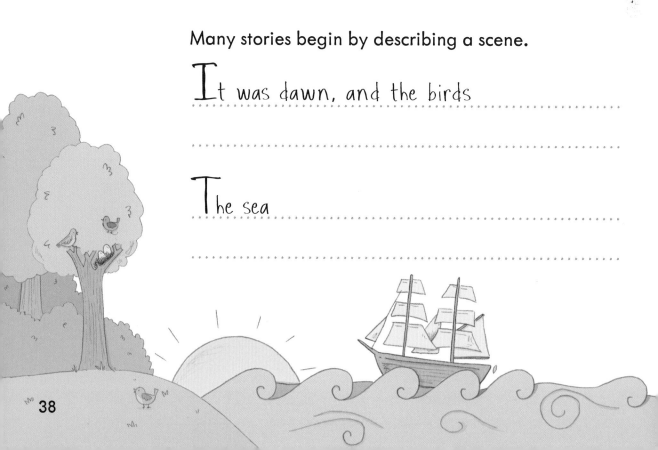

Stories can also begin with someone talking.
What might this person be saying?

"

....

....

....

"

These are speech
marks. Use them
to show someone
is talking.

BANG!

Some stories start with a dramatic event.
Write the first few lines of this story.

BANG! went the ....

....

....

....

....

CLANK!

In the middle

Fred the kitchen boy finds the King's crown. He needs to return it before the full moon, but it's a dangerous journey...

Beginning

Draw a line to take Fred to the King.
Fred's route can be as long
or short as you like!

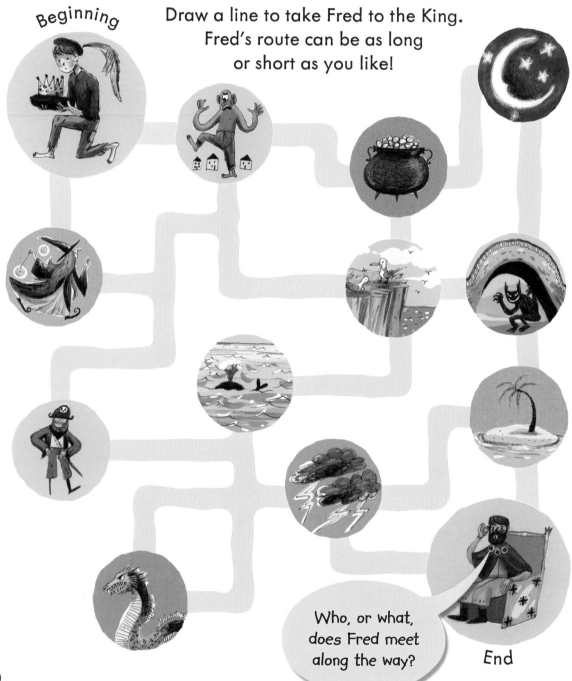

Who, or what, does Fred meet along the way?

End

Write about Fred's journey here – and make it sound exciting.

Along the way, Fred ....

....

....

....

....

....

....

....

....

....

Use words and phrases like these to link up the different parts of my journey.

Little did he know   As night fell

Luckily   Unfortunately   Suddenly

Without warning   While   As if by magic

Then   Before long   SURPRISINGLY

Endings

Stories often end with a problem being solved or a plan working out.

Match each of these story ideas with a likely ending.

Story ideas	Endings
Nancy's dream...	...is solved.
The evil emperor's plan...	...is a success.
Agent Z's secret mission...	...finds a way back to Earth.
The mystery of the disappearing hedgehog...	...is ruined.
The daring jungle explorers...	...finally comes true.
The astronaut stuck in space...	...arrive safely at their treehouse.

Try finishing off these last lines. You could make them funny, sad, touching or surprising.

They all lived ....

....

As for the dragon, ...

....?

Everything was perfect, apart from ....

....

The crowd roared when finally ....

....

....

WINNER!

never again   **at last**   just a dream   ...or did they?

happily ever after   **time for bed**   whatever happens   43

What's going on?

Imagine what toys get up to when no one else is around.

Make up a story about the toys and write it here.

Give your story a beginning, a middle and an ending.

....

....

....

You could begin with the toys coming to life.

....

....

....

What mischief do they get into?

....

....

What do they do when the children arrive home?

....

....

Here are some names and ideas to help you.

the Peg family   Steve Stegosaurus

dino makeover   abseiled   scatter

Suzy Sockmonkey   car chase   slinky

Choosing titles

Every story needs a title – something that suits it and helps it to stand out from the rest.

Here are some examples:

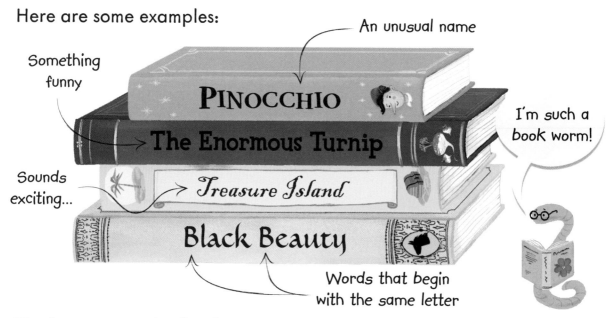

An unusual name

Something funny

PINOCCHIO

The Enormous Turnip

Sounds exciting...

Treasure Island

Black Beauty

Words that begin with the same letter

I'm such a book worm!

Think up some titles for these covers.

Here's a space for you to design your own cover.
Make the title clear and memorable,
and draw a picture to go with it.

Written by

Victory!

Imagine winning an important competition. It could be a sports event, a talent show, even a knights' tournament...

Name your competition here.

....

....

You'll never get the *ball* past me.

What challenges do you face?

....

....

....

....

....

....

How do you win in the end?

....

....

....

Now write the story
of your victory.

Foxed in Final

Give your
story an
interesting title.

....

....

....

....

....

....

....

....

....

....

The impossible
can become
possible in your
stories.

....

....

X meets Y

Choose two very different characters.
What happens when they meet?

Your characters can *be completely made up*...

...or they can *be from stories you already know.*

Who are your characters?

.... (X) and .... (Y)

Where do they meet?

....

What does X say?

....

What does Y say?

....

Something surprising or funny could happen.

What happens next?

....

flying mouse   Prince Talkalot   TV star

magician   wise old robot   Prime Minister

Snow White   TROLL   King Toad

Now write down their story.

Remember to give your story a beginning, a middle and an ending.

One day ....

....

....

....

....

....

....

....

....

....

....

A story plan

If you're writing a longer story, it helps to plan it out first.

Story plans are often split into five stages. Here's a plan for a story called...

The Enormous Turnip

1. Beginning

A farmer went to pick some turnips.

2. Build-up

He tried to pick the biggest turnip, but it wouldn't move.

3. Problem!

Even three people couldn't uproot it.

4. Solution

More helpers joined in. Finally they heaved the turnip out.

It's enormous!

5. Ending

They made enough soup from the turnip to last them a year.

Use the plan on the left to write your own version of the Enormous Turnip story.

You could make up names for the characters.

Add plenty of action and drama.

In stories, things often go wrong before they come right again.

Write a comic

Comics use words and pictures to tell a story.
The pictures for this comic have been drawn for you.
It's up to you to decide what the characters are saying.

Beginning

Look at all the
pictures before
you start writing.

Build-up

You don't need
to use speech
marks in speech
bubbles.

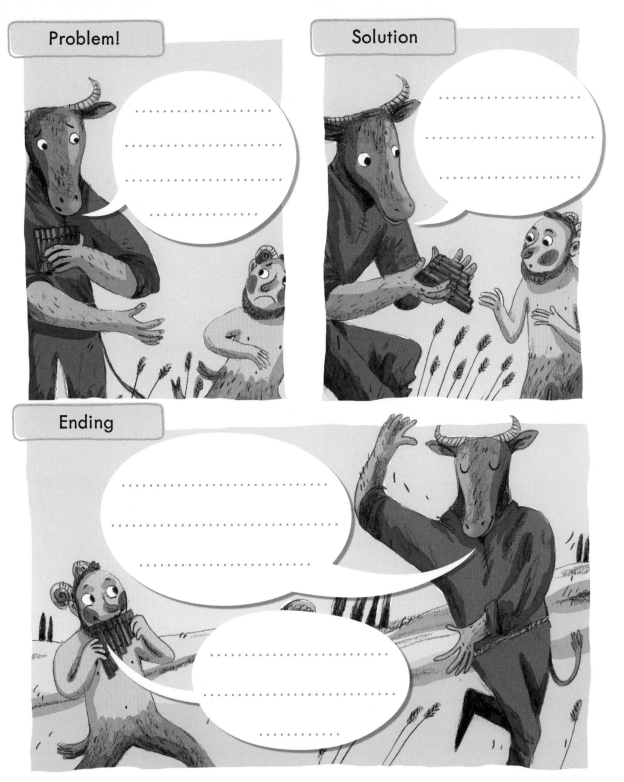

Eek!   I mean you no harm.   Here you go.   Oops!

Don't be scared.   I love this tune.   Help, a monster!

Your very own story

Use these boxes to plan out your own story,
then turn to the next page and write it down.

Beginning

....

....

....

....

....

Introduce your
main characters
and describe
where they are.

Build-up

....

....

....

....

....

What are your
characters doing?
Are they facing
a challenge?

For help coming
up with ideas,
turn to page 60.

Problem!

....
....
....
....
....

What goes wrong?

Solution

How do things get better?

....
....
....
....
....

Ending

....
....
....
....
....

How does it work out in the end?

Give your story a title.

....

....

....

....

....

....

....

....

....

....

....

....

....

....

? ! " " , .

Ideas generator

Story ideas can come from books, movies, real life or anywhere. Use these two pages for some extra inspiration.

Who?

lucky child

mysterious inventor

helpful fairy

naughty dog

haughty queen

jolly knight

sleepy horse

my toothbrush

a speeding car

What?

a missing boot

whiff

a ghostly galleon

Granny's false teeth

an ancient riddle

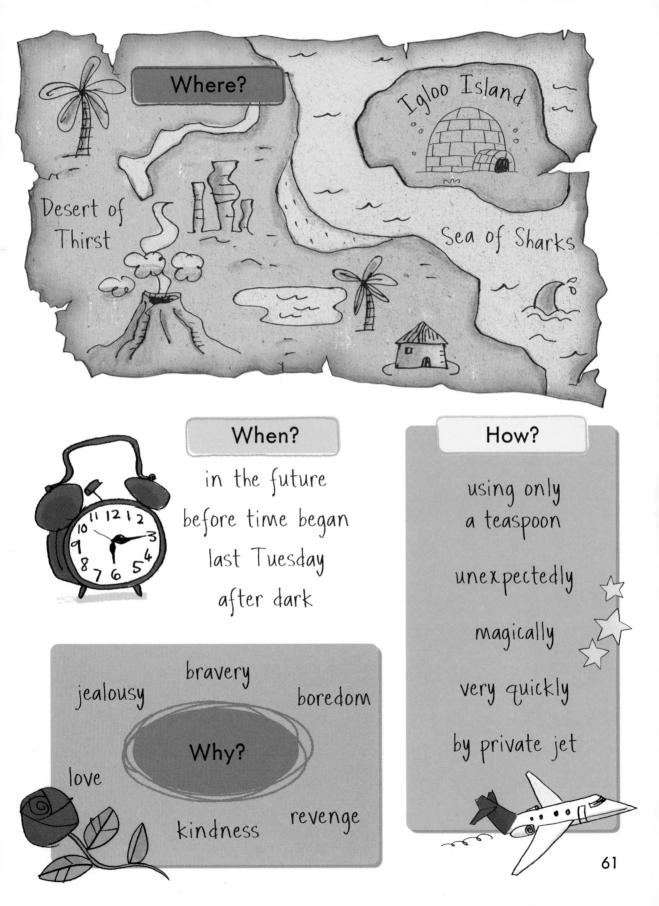

Where?

Igloo Island

Desert of Thirst

Sea of Sharks

When?

in the future
before time began
last Tuesday
after dark

How?

using only
a teaspoon

unexpectedly

magically

very quickly

by private jet

bravery

jealousy

boredom

Why?

love

kindness

revenge

Word hoard

Whenever you come across an exciting word, you can write it down here.

FIERCE

majestic

FIERY

shimmer

gnarled

extravagant

flounce

leap

shuffle

....

....

....

....

....

....

....

....

....

....

....

....

stroke

thrilled

tremble

Credits

This is where everyone involved in this book gets mentioned.

AUTHOR

. . . .

. . . .

Write your own name in as the author.

WRITING TIPS & IDEAS

Katie Daynes and Louie Stowell

ILLUSTRATORS

Briony May Smith, Jen Hill, Rachel Stubbs, Fred Blunt and Natasha Rimmington

DESIGNERS

Hayley Wells and Laura Wood

EDITOR

Ruth Brocklehurst

LITERACY EXPERT

Dr. Kerenza Ghosh

ON THE INTERNET:

There are lots of amazing websites with helpful story writing ideas.

Go to the Usborne Quicklinks website at www.usborne.com/quicklinks and type in 'story writing' to find out more.

Please ask your parent or guardian before using the internet.

We recommend that children are supervised while on the internet. Please read our safety guidelines at the Usborne Quicklinks website.